Curious George ®

Plumber's Helper

Adaptation by Marcy Goldberg Sacks and Priya Giri Desai
Based on the TV series teleplay written by Joe Fallon

Houghton Mifflin Harcourt
Boston New York 2010

For information about permission to reproduce selections from this book, write to Permissions, Houghton Mifflin Harcourt Publishing Company, 215 Park Avenue South, New York, New York 10003.

Library of Congress Cataloging-in-Publication data is on file.
ISBN: 978-0-547-23589-9

Design by Afsoon Razavi and Marcy Goldberg Sacks
www.hmhbooks.com
Manufactured in Malaysia
TWP 10 9 8 7 6 5 4 3 2 1

George loved bath time. Today he had a good idea. He took a box of new toys into the bath with him.

But these toys didn't float like his usual
bath toys. With bath time over, George pulled the
stopper. All the water went down the drain. And so did his toys!

George thought hard. Since the toys went away when the water drained, maybe they would come back up if he filled the tub again. George turned the bathtub faucet. Uh-oh. Water began to pour from the sink instead.

Water was backing up in every sink in the apartment, even in the kitchen!
"What's going on?" wondered the man with the yellow hat. It was time to
call the plumber.

Mr. Auger, the plumber, arrived. From the plunger
in his tool belt to the wrenches in his toolbox,
Mr. Auger had some of the best tools George had ever seen.

George went with Mr. Auger to the basement, where the pipes were. "Some pipes bring water in, and some take water out," Mr. Auger explained.

"This main valve turns water on and off for the whole building," he told George. Mr. Auger used a wrench to close the main valve. "Now that the water is turned off," he explained, "we can check inside the pipes in your apartment to find the clog that is causing the problem."

Then Mr. Auger showed George how to remove a pipe joint and drain the bathroom sink. George peeked inside the pipe. Mr. Auger looked too, but he didn't find a clog.

Mr. Auger unscrewed pipes in the kitchen, and using his screwdriver, he found the clog—George's toys! But how did they get from the bathroom to the kitchen?

Mr. Auger explained that water from the bath pushed the toys down the pipes until the toy snake got tangled up and stuck.

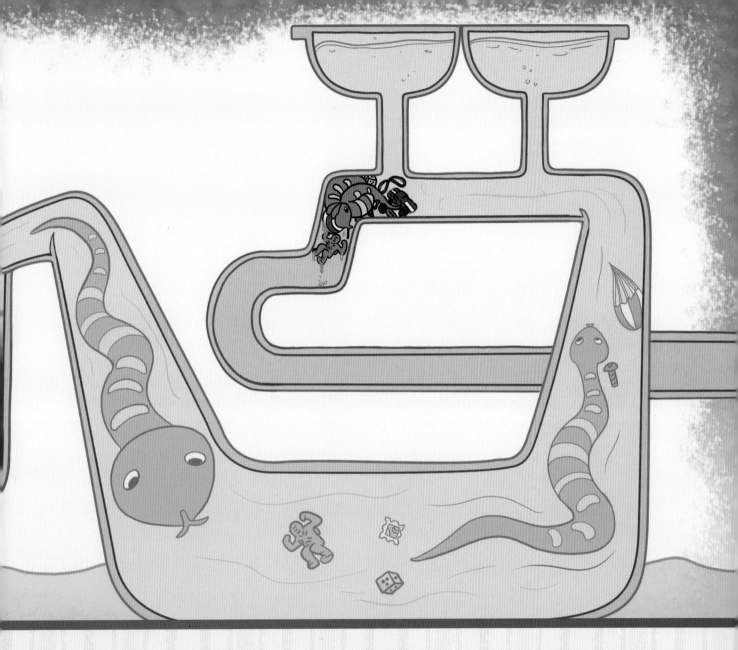

The other toys got stuck in the same spot too. The water couldn't get through, so it started going up other pipes and out into the sinks.

After Mr. Auger tightened the pipes in the apartment, he let George open the main valve in the basement. George couldn't believe it—now he knew how to fix a clogged drain too!

After lunch the next day, the man asked George to clean up because he had to go out. "Make sure to dump the food out before you wash the dishes in the dishwasher," he reminded George as he left. So George poured the food down the dishwasher drain.

After loading all of the dishes, George started the dishwasher. Water and bubbles started oozing out of the machine!

George decided there must be a new clog in the pipes. He swung into action. Using his monkey tools, he closed the main valve in the basement, just like Mr. Auger.

George unscrewed the pipes and checked for clogs, but he didn't find anything. Maybe the clog was gone.

George reopened the main valve in the basement. But upstairs, the dishwasher was still overflowing.

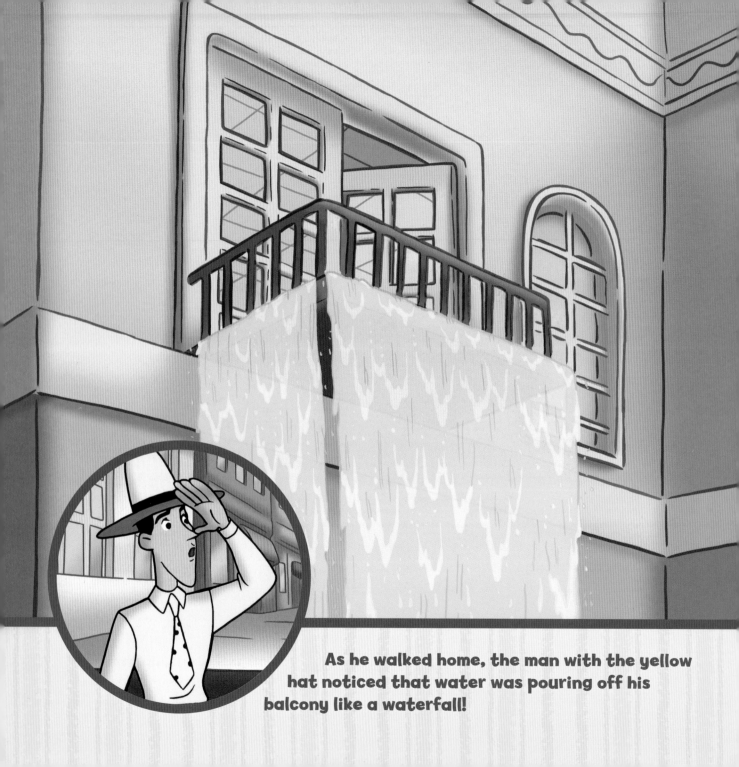

As he walked home, the man with the yellow hat noticed that water was pouring off his balcony like a waterfall!

The man called the plumber right away! "The food clogged the dishwasher just like your toys clogged the pipes," Mr. Auger said.
George finally understood: only liquids should go down the drain.

That night when George took his bath, he didn't have to worry about
clogging the pipes. His new bath toy was too big to go down the drain!

Water Works

Where Does Your Water Comes From?

Water can get to your home from two sources: surface water (water from rain, lakes, and rivers), or ground water (water from wells). This water is made safe to drink in treatment centers or home filter systems before it travels through several pipes to get to your home. When you are finished with the water, it either ends up in a holding tank to evaporate back into the air, or it travels through pipes to a treatment center to be cleaned and used for other things.

Where Are All of the Pipes?

Take a tour of your house. What are all of the things that are connected to pipes? Make a list of the things you find using the lines below.

-     -   -

-     -   -

-     -   -

POSSIBLE ANSWERS: sink, dishwasher, washing machine, shower, toilet, hose.

Tool Time

With the tools below, George is ready to tackle any plumbing problem! Color George in his fix-it outfit, and then label all of the different tools. Ask an adult if you don't know the name of a tool.

1. - - - - - - - - - - - - -

2. - - - - - - - - - - - - -

3. - - - - - - - - - - - - -

4. - - - - - - - - - - - - -

5. - - - - - - - - - - - - -

6. - - - - - - - - - - - - -

Answers: 1. pipe joint 2. faucet handle 3. screwdriver 4. hammer 5. plunger 6. wrench